Lampreys to Robots

Tech from Nature

By Jennifer Colby

21st Century
Junior Library

Published in the United States of America by
Cherry Lake Publishing
Ann Arbor, Michigan
www.cherrylakepublishing.com

Reading Adviser: Marla Conn, MS, Ed., Literacy specialist, Read-Ability, Inc.
Content Adviser: Rachel Brown, MA, Sustainable Business

Photo Credits: © Theresa Grace/Shutterstock.com, Cover, 1 [left]; © Photo Oz/Shutterstock.com, Cover, 1 [right];
© Monkey Business Images/Shutterstock.com, 4; © Dean Drobot/Shutterstock.com, 6; © sportpoint/Shutterstock.com, 8;
© steve estvanik/Shutterstock.com, 10; © Morphart Creation/Shutterstock.com, 12; © U.S. Department of Energy/
Flickr, 14; © U.S. Fish and Wildlife Service, 16; © jack perks/Shutterstock.com, 18; © socrates471/Shutterstock.com, 20

Library of Congress Cataloging-in-Publication Data

Names: Colby, Jennifer, 1971– author.
Title: Lampreys to robots / Jennifer Colby.
Description: Ann Arbor : Cherry Lake Publishing, [2019] | Series: Tech from nature | Audience: Grade 4 to 6. |
   Includes bibliographical references and index.
Identifiers: LCCN 2018035556 | ISBN 9781534142978 (hardcover) | ISBN 9781534139534 (pbk.) |
   ISBN 9781534140738 (pdf) | ISBN 9781534141933 (hosted ebook)
Subjects: LCSH: Artificial limbs—Juvenile literature. | Prosthesis—Juvenile literature. | Lampreys—Juvenile literature. |
   Biomimicry—Juvenile literature.
Classification: LCC RD756 .C54 2019 | DDC 617.5/8—dc23
LC record available at https://lccn.loc.gov/2018035556

Cherry Lake Publishing would like to acknowledge the work of the Partnership for 21st Century Skills.
Please visit *www.p21.org* for more information.

Printed in the United States of America
Corporate Graphics

CONTENTS

Robotics can help people who have lost a limb.

Robotic Help

Have you ever seen a person who is missing an arm or a leg? Robot science helps these people. The field researches ways to improve **artificial limbs**. These limbs help people move more easily.

You can still be active and live a normal life with an artificial limb.

Living Without a Limb

People lose limbs in accidents. They could also lose limbs from a disease. Though these events can be **tragic**, there are medical **devices** that can help. A person who loses an arm or a leg might choose to have a **prosthetic** limb. These devices help people lead an easier life.

It is easier to run with a modern prosthetic limb.

Prosthetic limbs have changed over the years. The study of eel-like fish called lampreys has improved prosthetic arms and legs. How is this possible? Let's take a closer look.

Ask Questions!

Do you know anybody who has a prosthetic arm or leg? If the person is willing to talk about it, ask questions about his or her day-to-day life. Compare it to how you live your life. Are there any differences?

Lampreys can live in both seawater and freshwater.

It's Alive!

Scientists in Chicago used a lamprey to guide a robot! They removed a lamprey's nervous system, which includes the brain and spinal cord. Then they attached these parts to a small robot. They studied the connection between the lamprey's simple nervous system and the robot.

The lamprey-powered robot, named Khepera, is able to move on its own. It can direct itself to move in circular patterns. The **biomedical engineers** hope to use the

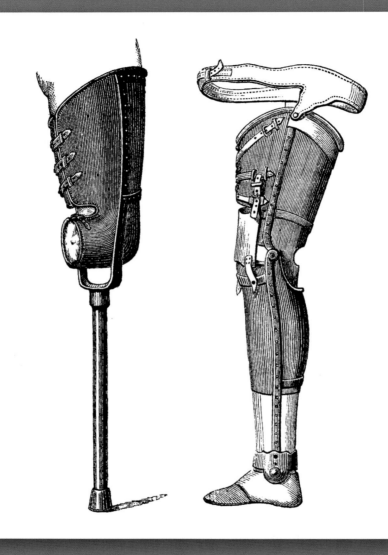

Early prosthetic legs were clunky and made of wood and leather.

science behind the lamprey robot to make robotic limbs for patients. Their work is based on the concept of **biomimicry**. Biomimicry is a rapidly growing scientific field of research.

Early artificial limbs usually did not bend and were very uncomfortable to wear. In the early 1500s, a French doctor invented **hinged** prosthetic limbs that attached more securely to the body.

Advances in medicine have allowed doctors to perform more careful **amputation** surgeries. This means that **amputees** can have better connections to new artificial limbs. Connections such as suction cups

A modern artificial limb has many parts.

and permanent implants allow for more natural movement.

Today's artificial limbs are more advanced. Plastics and **carbon fiber** make modern prosthetics stronger, more flexible, and more realistic.

But there is room for improvement. Think about the biomedical engineers and their experiments with the lamprey's nervous system. It is a self-guided robot! Their work could make artificial limbs more lifelike.

Make a Guess!

What is it about the lamprey that makes it useful for developing prosthetic devices? Write down your guesses. Read on and compare your guesses to the answers in the next chapter. Were you close?

Lampreys depend on other fish for survival.

Investigating Nature

The lamprey is a jawless fish. It is also a parasite. A parasite is an animal that lives on or in the body of another animal. The lamprey survives by attaching itself to other fish and sucking their blood. Like many other parasites, it has a simple nervous system. This allows scientists to easily study and experiment with the lamprey.

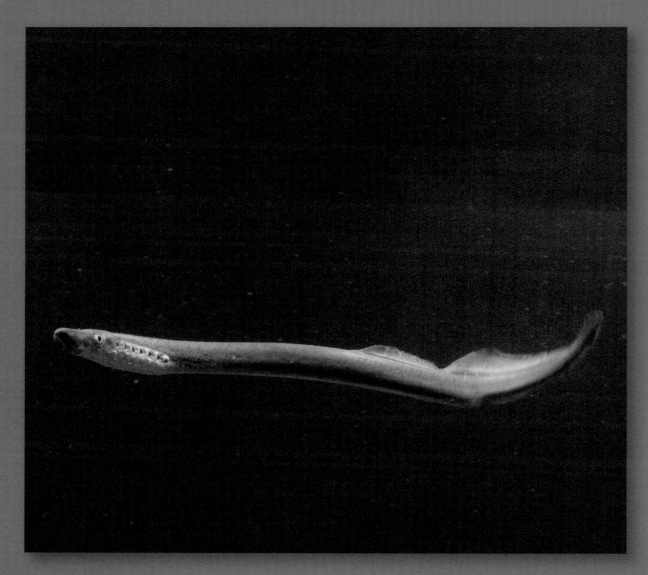

Lampreys swim easily in the water.

For the Khepera robot, the researchers connected **sensors** on the robot to the lamprey's **brain stem**. Then they made **impulses**, similar to the impulses we make in our brains, from the lamprey's spinal cord to direct the movement of the robot's wheels. This type of robot could be used to control all kinds of devices.

Think!

Why do you think scientists study lampreys for developing prosthetic limbs? Why not other parasites? Use the internet and your library to research other types of parasites. Compare the different types.

The human brain could control an artificial limb.

The study of lampreys controlling a robot influences new and better prosthetics. Understanding the lamprey's special **anatomy** could help scientists create robotic limbs for amputees that respond to the human brain.

Look!

It's not just humans that benefit from prosthetic limbs. Animals do, too! Ask a librarian to help you find more information about animals and prosthetic limbs. Are there ways these prosthetic limbs can be improved?

GLOSSARY

amputation (am-pyoo-TAY-shun) a medical treatment in which a doctor cuts off a damaged or diseased part of the patient's body

amputees (am-pyoo-TEEZ) people who have had an amputation surgery

anatomy (uh-NAT-uh-mee) the parts that form a living thing

artificial (ahr-tuh-FISH-uhl) not natural, created by humans

biomedical engineers (bye-oh-MED-ih-kuhl en-juh-NEERZ) people who design and build medical products with the natural sciences in mind

biomimicry (bye-oh-MIM-ik-ree) copying plants and animals to build or improve something

brain stem (BRAYN STEM) the part of the brain that connects to the spinal cord

carbon fiber (KAHR-buhn FAHY-ber) a strong lightweight man-made material

devices (dih-VISE-ez) objects, machines, or pieces of equipment that have been made for some special purpose

hinged (HINJD) a joint that allows something to bend

impulses (IM-puhls-ez) small amounts of energy that move from one area to another

limbs (LIMZ) legs or arms

prosthetic (pros-THET-ik) an artificial device that is designed to replace a body part that is missing

sensors (SEN-serz) devices that detect or sense things like heat, light, sound, motion, and then react to it in a particular way

tragic (TRAJ-ik) serious and sad